IMAGES OF ENGLAND

BARTON HILL
REVISITED

YOU ARE NOW ENTERING
BARTON HILL
HAVE A NICE STAY

IMAGES OF ENGLAND

BARTON HILL
REVISITED

BARTON HILL HISTORY GROUP

TEMPUS

Frontispiece: Barton Hill Rules – OK?

First published 2005

Tempus Publishing Limited
The Mill, Brimscombe Port,
Stroud, Gloucestershire, GL5 2QG
www.tempus-publishing.com

© Barton Hill History Group, 2005

The right of Barton Hill History Group to be identified as the
Author of this work has been asserted in accordance with the
Copyrights, Designs and Patents Act 1988.

British Library Cataloguing in Publication Data.
A catalogue record for this book is available from the British Library.

ISBN 0 7524 3557 4

Typesetting and origination by Tempus Publishing Limited.
Printed in Great Britain.

Contents

Members of the committee of the Barton Hill Histoy Group, 2005. From left to right: Jean Brake, Andy Jones, Pauline Luscombe, Dave Cheesley, Doreen Parsons and Ernie Haste. Vice-Chairman Garry Atterton, not pictured, is also a contributor to this book.

Acknowledgements

The Barton Hill History Group wishes to thank all of its supporters over the past twenty-two years – it's been fun!

Regarding this book, we sincerely thank: Garry Atterton, John Bennett, Jean Brake, Tony Brake, John Calvin, the late Harold, Dancey, D.C.B. Dean, Roy Edwardes, Jack Fryer, George Gardiner, Reg Gregory, Harry Griffin, Ernie Haste, Peter Heaslip, Carrie Hitchcock, Mike Hooper, Hilda Jennings, Ray Knight, Pauline Luscombe, the late Samuel Loxton, Jim Morris, Mr Parker, Doreen Parsons, Ben Price, Alan Pruett, Ruth Shapcott, Beryl Smith, Dave Stephenson, Dot Tranter, John Williams, Jill Willmott, Barton Hill Settlement, Barton Hill Monday Group, Bristol Central Library, Bristol Evening Post, City Academy Bristol. And, of course, the inspiration of the late William Sanigar.

Special thanks go to the current Chairman of the BHHG, Andy Jones, and Group Secretary/Treasurer, David Cheesley, for their dedication and hard work in making this book possible.

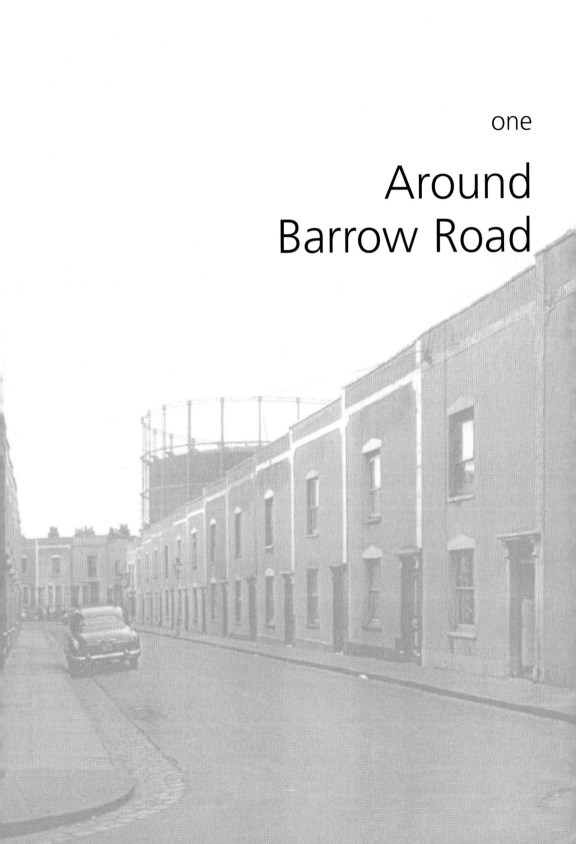

one

Around
Barrow Road

For many years the Barrow Road bit of Barton Hill presented a classic, urban working-class Victorian scene: rows of terraced houses, a mass of railway lines with bridges and, looming over it all, gigantic gas holders. Non conformist chapels and pubs occupied odd corners nestled between the houses. But in the 1960s all was to change for this community.

Unlike the central area of Barton Hill, Barrow Road was not targeted for new high-rise flats. However, Barrow Road, Digby Street and Bridge Street fell within the orbit of the proposed Outer Circuit Road, an urban motorway link between the Parkway (M32) and Totterdown. The closure of the Barrow Road loco shed in late 1965 was highly symbolic and soon a ghostly silence fell upon once vibrant streets and shops. Demolition followed gradually but steadily.

The new road did not materialise but new town houses were built. However, during 1980/81, the gas holders were pulled down, a new Days Road was constructed and commercial structures were built. In 1993 the landmark Barrow Road viaduct was swept away for the Spine Road (St Philips Causeway), a 1990s successor to the 1960s Outer Circuit Road.

Andy Jones, chairman of the Barton Hill History Group, recalls:
I went down there a lot when I got my bike, the best part of thirty years ago now. At this time Digby Street and Bridge Street were still there, technically. Not the streets of homes, families and neighbours but ghostly reminders of the past. If you stepped away from Barrow Road across a tangle of wild greenery and discarded rubbish, the roadways of Bridge Street and Digby Street could be 'discovered', hidden among a dense covering of weeds and litter. Odd bricks and tiles lying around were the only evidence that houses had once stood there. However the pavements were largely intact as were the actual carriageways. But it was difficult to picture that these 'old bits of road' were once the site of living, breathing streets.

As a youngster on my bike, this bit of Barton Hill was interesting, it was like a wild frontier; hidden roads, fragments from a demolished railway shed, a rather impressive viaduct, a ludicrously old-fashioned humpback bridge and this vast wasteland with maybe an abandoned Ford Corsair dumped among the weeds and rubbish. And towering over it all, the huge columns and lattice girders of the gas holders, spectacular landmarks and a tribute to Victorian engineering.

Dave Cheesley, secretary of the Barton Hill History Group, recalls:
In my memory there are two Barrow Roads; the first is the Barrow Road I knew in the 1950s and 1960s. This was the Barrow Road of community and railways. The Barrow Road of terraced houses, small shops and steam trains. On Saturday afternoons my grandmother would sometimes take me to Gaunts Ham Park, a great place to see steam trains. The swings were in the shadow of the giant coaling tower. Huddled below waiting to be coaled would be steam engines of all sizes and passing would be express trains racing north and south. Beyond the tower was the great thirteen-arch viaduct taking Barrow Road across the busy railway yards. The other good vantage point for trainspotting was the top of the steps that linked the viaduct with the shed yard.

The second is the Barrow Road I knew in the 1970s and 1980s. This was the Barrow Road of dereliction. The Barrow Road of weeds, rubbish and abandoned cars only disturbed by the occasional invasion by travellers and gypsies adding even more mess.

But both Barrow Roads had lasting character and memories that have now been replaced by the new Barrow Road of the Spine Road and industrial estates.

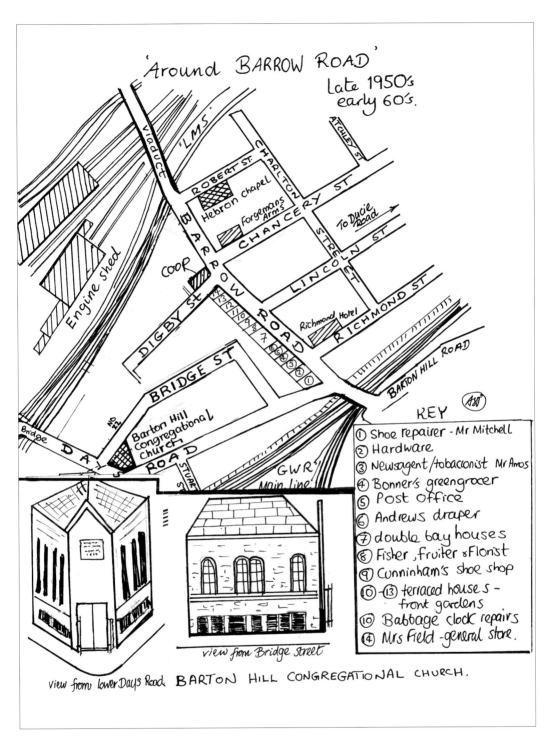

'Around BARROW ROAD'
Late 1950's early 60's.

KEY

① Shoe repairer - Mr Mitchell
② Hardware
③ Newsagent/tobacconist Mr Amos
④ Bonner's greengrocer
⑤ Post Office
⑥ Andrews draper
⑦ double bay houses
⑧ Fisher, Fruiter & Florist
⑨ Cunninham's shoe shop
⑩-⑬ terraced houses - front gardens
⑩ Babbage clock repairs
⑭ Mrs Field - general store.

view from lower Days Road   BARTON HILL CONGREGATIONAL CHURCH.

view from Bridge street

A map of the Barrow Road area, *c.* 1960.

You can almost smell the steam in this photograph. The last steam engines depart from Barrow Road shed on 20 November 1965. British Railways 9F–class freight locomotive 92209 and two ex–GWR 57XX–class pannier tanks leave Barrow Road for the last time.

It's hard to believe that this mass of wasteland was once a thriving railway yard. This is the scene in 1980. The thirteen-arch viaduct was to survive another thirteen years. The flats of Lawrence Hill and Easton dominate the skyline. On the extreme right is Berkeley House, then the new offices of the Bristol Omnibus Co., which replaced the old headquarters building at the Tramway Centre, St Augustine's Parade.

Hebron Methodist church, Barrow Road, with Robert Street off to the left. During demolition in 1977, a green bottle was found behind the foundation stone. It contained a newspaper for the day the stone was laid, 7 September 1868. Unfortunately water had entered the bottle and all that could be read was an advert for custard! The foundation stone and bottle were saved and incorporated into the warehouse which replaced the church.

The Forgeman's Arms on the corner of Chancery Street; a remarkable survivor. By 1980, when this picture was taken, it was the only surviving building from the old Barrow Road. Noted for its wood panelling and original leaded glass, it was a popular haunt of railwaymen from the nearby engine sheds.

Early 1965, looking towards the viaduct with Days Road off to the left. On the corner is Mitchell's shoe repair shop, part of a terrace of Edwardian shops which included the Barton Hill sub-post office. By 1973 this rank presented a sorry sight; boarded-up and awaiting demolition.

10 January 1982, wintry conditions at the same position seventeen years later. Note the Forgeman's Arms on the right and the viaduct straight ahead. The new Days Road/Barrow Road mini roundabout (to the left) was built in 1980. On the left, was the site of a large property referred to as Barton Hill House in 1828. This was one of a number of impressive country houses in old Barton Hill. It was demolished around 1904.

Right: The 1920s, Alfred, Reg and Daisy Long outside No. 52 Chancery Street. Reg Long was a doorman for many years at St Luke's church

Below: The 1920s, Chancery Street, outside No. 52. The gang includes some of the Longs.

The Barrow Road viaduct is sandwiched between the the Folly Lane gas holders and the 1965 Kingmarsh House tower block, 1967. The rest of the former Midland Railway land stands derelict.

Revealing panorama, 1968. The houses and shops of Barrow Road and Digby Street (centre left) contrast with the new 1960s houses. The railway cutting runs left to right. Cement wagons stand on one remaining line which ran down to the cement depot at Avonside. Note the different architectural styles and how the gas holders dominate the landscape.

Looking across the railway cutting to 'the desert' which had been Richmond, Lincoln and Chancery Streets, 1966. The large 1930s LMS coaling tower awaits demolition. It was blown up by explosives early one Sunday morning. Note the large number of trucks and locos to the left of the viaduct. Across the 'thirteen arches', the houses of Newtown await demolition.

Two years later, in 1968, the new three-storey town houses were built around Arthur Skemp Close, William Mason Close and Ernest Barker Close. All three were named after prominent figures in the early work of Barton Hill's University Settlement. Dr Skemp, Professor of English, was a distinguished and popular Settlement leader. An officer during the First World War, he was tragically killed in action on 1 November 1918.

Hickery's butchers shop, Barrow Road, seen here in around 1930, was in the terrace between Lincoln Street and Richmond Street.

The Co-op at Nos 90-92 Barrow Road. This popular shop was situated on the corner of Digby Street. Opened in 1927, it provided a working family's everyday needs at a minimum cost. Any profits were returned to its customers with the Co-op dividend. Like many Co-op stores it used an elaborate but effective 'wire and shuttle system' for handling cash. Its closure in 1967 marked the end for the old Barrow Road.

The Richmond Hotel on the corner of Richmond Street, 1965. This fine three-storey building was built in the 1870s. On the other corner of the street was a fish and chip shop known to all as Kitty's. Across Barrow Road from the Richmond Hotel was a row of shops that catered for most of the locals' daily needs. Note the police communication pillar.

Taken from almost the same position as the previous photograph, but three years later, a new 1960s landscape which the Richmond Hotel, unlike the Forgeman's Arms, didn't make it in to. When built, the new houses were known as the Gaunts Park housing estate.

Left: The May Festival, Lincoln Street, 1934. The houses dated from the 1860s–70s building expansion in East Bristol. Lincoln Street was a 'long 'un', containing over 110 houses plus two beer retailers: the Engineer's Arms and the Lion. There were also a number of shopkeepers and a fish and chip shop on the corner of Charlton Street.

Below: Richmond Street looking towards Ducie Road, 1965. This scene of empty streets with boarded-up houses was familiar over many parts of Barton Hill, Newtown and Easton at this time. Demolition, of what the council saw as grey, monotonous and outdated dwellings, was imminent.

A busy scene at the Barrow Road shed with the tall houses of Digby Street in the background, October 1964.

Lifting the track, the view from the Days Road humpback bridge, 1967. The engine shed had been demolished the year before but Digby Street on the right lingers on. Note Hebron Chapel in the background. The old humpback bridge was demolished in 1981 and a year later plans were unveiled for a transfer refuse station. This was eventually built on part of the derelict railway land.

Digby Street seen from Bridge Street, 1967. This dead-end street was made up of five different terraces of houses. The four-storey houses were unique in Barton Hill. They had tremendous views over the sprawling railway lines of the Barrow Road shed and Midland main line.

Days Road looking to the junction with Barrow Road, July 1980. The houses on both sides of this road had all gone by 1972. The site of Bridge Street was off left, but for ten years had been rough ground. This section of Days Road was closed forever a week after this picture was taken and a new highway was built off to the left.

Bridge Street, 1965. In the distance, opposite Bridge Street church, the houses were larger then those seen on the right. The 'big houses' had nine rooms (including basement), bay windows and front gardens with railings and tall stone pillars. Between the two types of houses, Mrs Lear ran an off-licence called the Ale & Porter stores. Bridge Street's houses were demolished between 1966 and 1970. However, the roadway was not removed until 1981.

Jean Brake in the garden of her family home, No. 22 Bridge Street, Barton Hill. Number 22 was one of Bridge Street's big houses (see above). In the background is the shed used by Art Sperring, a fruit and veg 'roundsman'. Overshadowing the whole scene are gas holders.

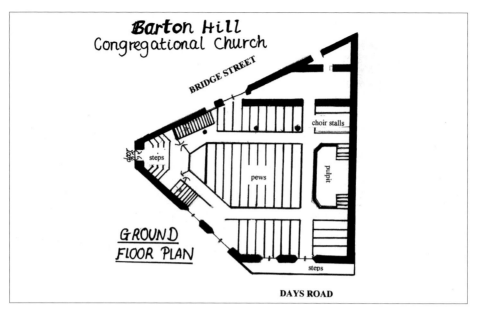

Above and below: Barton Hill Congregational church (see map p9). Founded in 1874 these drawings represent plans from 1905 when alterations were made to the building. The church closed in January 1968 and was purchased for demolition in August of that year. Mr White, church secretary, said at the time: 'for nearly 100 years this church has served a useful purpose but now town and country planning has taken its toll of churches and missions in Barton Hill for about the last time.'

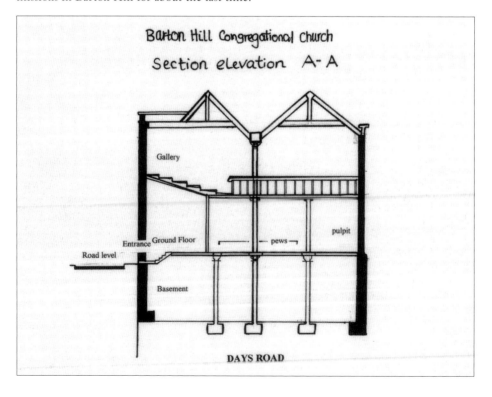

George V Silver Jubilee street party, Chancery Street, 1935. Chancery Street was a 'no thoroughfare' with the backs of the houses of Elizabeth Street at one end. On the corner with Atchley Street was a public house with the distinctive name the Leopard. Chancery Street still remains today but all its Victorian houses (including the Leopard) had been pulled down by 1966.

Gaunts Ham Park (popularly known as Lincoln Park) looking towards the Barrow Road viaduct, 1965. The LMS coaling tower can be glimpsed through the trees. In 1887 the council devoted this small two-acre 'pleasure and recreation ground' to serve the 'crowded district' of Barton Hill. It was significantly remodelled in 2004.

Barrow Road is somewhere between the houses and the weeds, on the afternoon of 22 July 1980. Part of the roadway of Bridge Street can just be glimpsed on the extreme right.

Stuart Street, 1993. Originally Stuart Street was a 'no thoroughfare' of nine houses leading from Days Road. The 'new' Stuart Street, an extension of the original, was built in 1980 to link (briefly) the old Days Road humpback bridge with the new Days Road extension. In the distance can be seen the Spine Road under construction which was to totally transform this viewpoint.

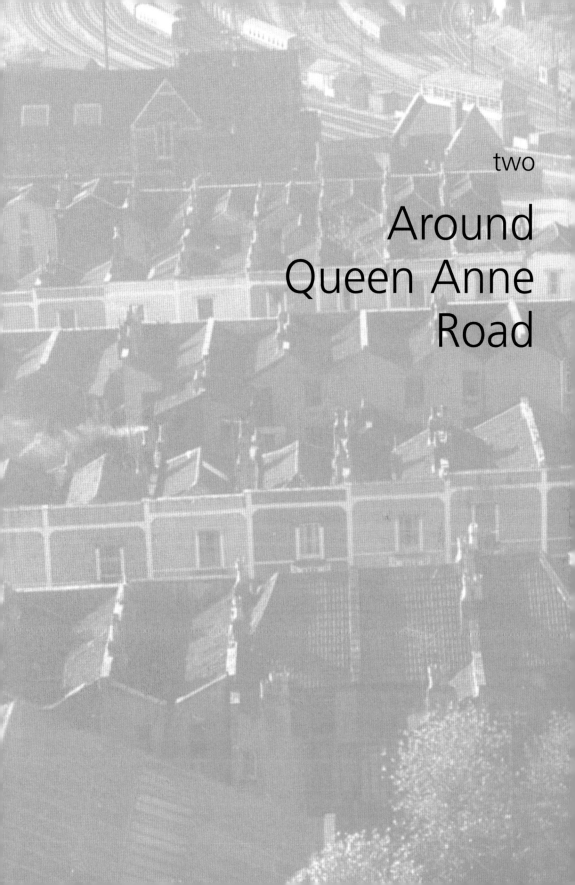

two

Around
Queen Anne
Road

The Council came along and decided half of the streets should go. They pulled down half of Beaconsfield Street, half of Canterbury Street and half of Holmes Street. Then for some reason they stopped at the rest. (*Jim Morris, born at No. 19 Beaconsfield Street*).

In 1968, two years after the last Barton Hill tower block was opened, the Queen Anne Road area of Barton Hill remained largely intact. The 'turkey field streets', and the earlier 1870/80s houses around Winstanley Street, seemed to have defied the bulldozers which had transformed Barton Hill in the 1950s. The council may have abandoned the 'adventure of high-rise living' but had not forgotten its desire to remove 'working-class housing' built before 1880 – the key year as far as redevelopment was concerned. As 1970 dawned so did the demolition crews and they headed for Winstanley Street, Ranelagh Street, Meyrick Street, Strode Street and Queen Anne Road. A sizeable chunk of this part of Barton Hill would soon disappear. A community of people would be moved out.

In the 1870s the United Land Co. Ltd acquired a large area of land to the west of the Great Western Cotton factory to build a new Barton Hill estate. The area was known as 'the turkey fields', a name originating from the turkey rhubarb which was grown on the site. In mid-Victorian times the scene was still decidedly rural in nature. This was an area of wheat fields, meadows, pleasant gardens and orchards. There were a few notable buildings, one being the Rhubarb Tavern which stood adjacent to the Barton Hill pottery. Opposite was a landmark in the area, a rambling country dwelling known as Queen Anne House or Tilly's Court. The thoughfare between the tavern and the house was described as the 'Lane leading from Barton Hill to St Philips glasshouses'. At the top end (towards the cotton works) was Barton Villa, another substantial residence with extensive gardens.

A significant year in Barton Hill's history was 1875, when the Bristol School Board built a new school in Jarvis Street. The 'lane to St Philips' became known as Queen Anne Road after its notable house.

To the south of the new road, the turkey fields were marked out for new building plots. However, development was slow and work didn't really start on the new houses until the surveyor A.W.W. Goulter promoted favourable building terms for the area.

In 1881 work stared on a new street in the turkey fields. A rank of standard terraced houses was built, and Holmes Street came into being. As was traditional in Victorian times, streets were not instant creations. They evolved over a number of years and often involved a number of different builders, each completing various plots in the street. Homes Street was not completed until 1895 when the 'southern side' was erected.

Back to Jim Morris:
On the corner of Canterbury Street was Jones' off-licence which later became Emery's. On the other side of Canterbury Street was Ruth Spear's shop. She sold milk, sweets and lemonade. She also had a milk round and she pushed a cart with two big wheels and a can in the middle of it. She later bought herself a Ford Prefect for her rounds.

The shop on the corner of Queen Anne Road and Goulter Street was run by Mr Fudge and had the name Live and Let Live. Like many corner shops in the area it was an off-licence and general store. Another general shop was Purnell's at the bottom of Holmes Street.

At the bottom of Goulter Street, top of Salisbury Street, was Price's Bakery. They sold their cakes off at the end of the day in bags. They were a good buy.

Unlike central Barton Hill, the Queen Anne Road area didn't get tower blocks and the demolitions seemed rather random. The area was not part of the original Barton Hill Redevelopment Area and having survived the massive demolition of the 1950s the erasing of the streets around Winstanley Street seemed a particular loss. Many substantial buildings were lost; these were not the basic 'cotton factory' dwellings of the 1840s. Some may recall the residents of Strode Street who resisted the bulldozers. Eventually only one house remained, its owners defiantly resisting the authorities. It remained totally isolated until it too came down and Strode Street was covered by the grass of the new school playing field.

Last words to Jim Morris:
I look back over those years with very fond memories as I remember all those people.

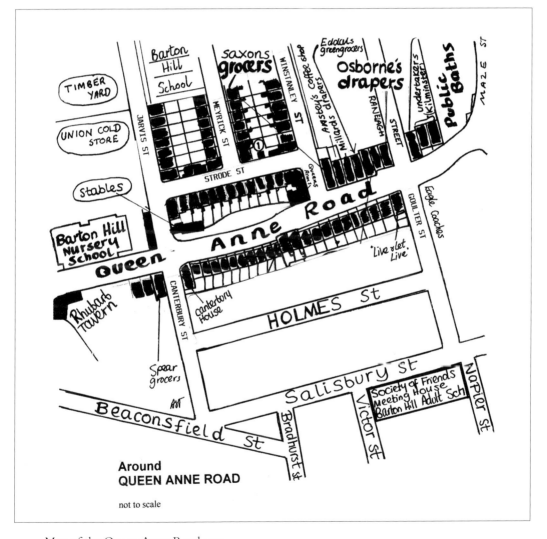

Map of the Queen Anne Road area.

The Rhubarb Tavern. This picture shows the Victorian red-brick extension which was added to the original farmhouse. Off to the right is a lane running alongside the pub garden. Until the 1880s this was the site of a terrace of houses called Queen Anne Street. It was demolished to accommodate the railway embankment. The new Ford Cortina Mark 4 and the Watney's 'Red Barrel' sign place this photo firmly in the 1970s.

Queen Anne Road, 1964. The houses in the distance had all been pulled down by 1971. Next to the Rhubarb Tavern are the houses which replaced the Barton Hill pottery. This was quite a large concern in the mid-Victorian period. It was the pottery of James Duffett, a significant Barton Hill landowner and industrialist. Note the fine selection of classic British-built cars.

Surviving until 1894, Tilly's Court was seen worthy enough for the Bristol illustrator Samuel Loxton to draw this picture. When built it would have been deep in the countryside. Although the precise historical development is not clear, it probably originated in the Tudor period. It acquired the name Queen Anne House, because of a local legend that the Stuart monarch stayed there as a guest of its owner Sir Thomas Day. As was common, the actual house was surrounded by a number of ancillary buildings.

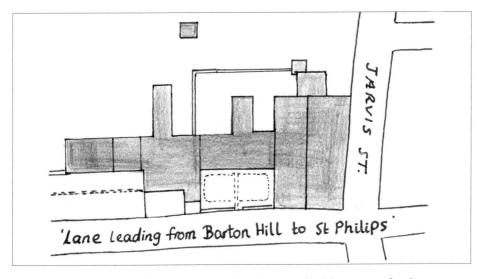

A plan of Tilly's Court in the mid-1880s. When it was pulled down, two fireplaces were saved. One went to Greenbank school, the other surviving one went just across the road to the Rhubarb Tavern. The interior of the house was probably very attractive with oak panelling and fine plasterwork.

The Barton Hill nursery and infants' school. This structure replaced Tilly's Court in 1895. Architecturally its red-brick Dutch design contrasted with the gothic style of nearby Jarvis Street school. On the corner behind the road sign was the grocer's shop of Ruth Spear.

Children of Winstanley Street plus their Jack Russell. This is apparently outside No. 5, which was at the Barton Hill Road end of the street. In the 1930s there was a fish and chip shop in Winstanley Street, Iles on the corner of Strode Street. By the mid-1950s the fish and chip shop had gone, replaced by Sta-tex dry cleaners. By 1965 this had become a wool shop.

The Canterbury House, on the corner of Queen Anne Road and Canterbury Street. This was a traditional off-licence, all the beers being drawn from 'the wood.' The barrels were ranged along the back walls on timber stands, covered with clean white covers. As with many such establishments, cooked meats were often sold. Mr Jones, who played water polo at Barton Hill Swimming Club was licensee for a number of years, followed in its last years by Mr and Mrs Emery. The Canterbury House was demolished in the mid-1960s, although the site was not built on for over twenty years!

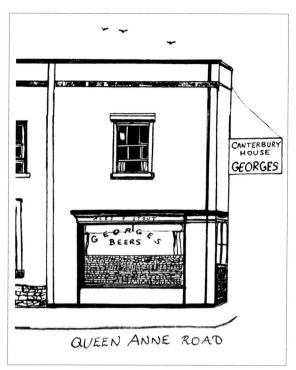

Looking towards the Rhubarb Tavern, 1977. By this time demolition on both sides had totally changed the character of Queen Anne Road. The car on the left is Japanese, which would have been unheard of in 1965!

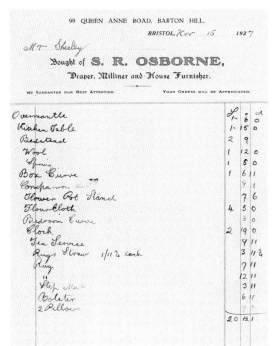

A receipt from S.R. Osborne, draper, milliner and house furnisher, who was on the corner of Queen Anne Road and Ranelagh Street. The shop was run in its latter years by Mrs Mabel Osborne. It had closed by 1966.

Sketch of some of the shops on Queen Anne Road which vanished in the 1960s. Numbers 93 and 95 were in the rank between Winstanley Street and Ranelagh Street. Applin's had been Stan Britton's tobacconist in the 1930s. These shops were formed by building on the front gardens of houses along the road. They were pulled down for the 1975 Barton Hill primary school.

A class at Barton Hill Nursery School, 1975.

St Luke's procession heads up Meyrick Street, *c.* 1946. The school buildings are on the right. As with other Barton Hill streets, the decision to pull down Meyrick Street came as a shock to many. For older residents especially, it often meant giving up a lifetime's association with friends and neighbours.

Jarvis Street looking towards Queen Anne Road, 1965. In this year the technical school (Building Department), which used the 1875 school buildings seen in the picture, closed. The technical school had been established in 1943 under the guidance of Mr Cole (followed by Mr Green in 1959). No further use was found for the old school buildings and in 1971 the Education Committee decided that they should be pulled down.

Opposite above: Barton Hill Rugby Football Club 1923/24. The Club will celebrate its 100th anniversary in 2008. The club's badge has the initials WERH as part of the design, the initials of its founder William Harris seen here standing on the extreme left. William E.R. Harris was one of Barton Hill's most respected characters. Born in 1875, he was the history teacher and sports master at Barton Hill school from 1908 to his retirement in 1935. Known affectionately as Billy or 'Tubby' Harris he is remembered for his sporting achievements at Barton Hill. He was coach of Barton Hill Swimming Club and Barton Hill Water Polo Team. In 1908 he founded Barton Hill Old Boys' Rugby Football Club. He won many trophies with all these teams. The club these days play at Duncombe Lane, Speedwell, where they have their own clubhouse.

Opposite below: Barton Hill Rugby Football Club, 1940s.

The occupants of No. 43 Winstanley Street stand proudly outside their property. These houses were superior to many in Barton Hill as they possessed bay windows and a small front garden. Winstanley Street was one of the last streets to be demolished in Barton Hill.

QUEENS ARMS

The Queens Arms, on the corner of Queen Anne Road and Winstanley Street. A relatively large, distinctive building which was an off-licence for nearly 100 years. In the 1920s it was run by the Howe family. In its latter days it was occupied by Mr William Davidge. Architecturally, the Queens Arms was quite an impressive structure.

This aerial shot shows the houses of respectively Ranelagh, Winstanley and Meyrick Streets, 1965. Top left is Jarvis Street school, while top right can be seen the Barrow Road/Days Road junction. Ten years later they had all gone!

Salisbury Street looking towards Price's bakery. The former adult school is on the right, on the corner of Napier Street. This 1890s street was named after the Prime Minister of the day, Lord Salisbury.

This structure, now the Community At Heart building in Salisbury Street, was originally the Bristol Friends First Day school. Built in 1899, the building was extended six years later to include a billiard room, skittle alley and gym. In the 1970s and '80s it was used by the Boys' Brigade, the Shaftesbury Crusade and the Barton Hill History Group.

Barton Hill Sunday school, Salisbury Street, going off to camp at Brean, 1947/48.

Barton Hill Sunday school camp was held at Hicks Farm for two weeks each year. Jim Morris recalls: 'we were looked after very well and the food was good. The tents leaked a bit but we had a good time. I still remember it clearly. Mr Wooley ran the camp and his son ran a club in the evening.'

Later Barton Hill Sunday school camp at Brean.

Arsenal and England legend Eddie Hapgood, left-back (1927-45), stands proudly as his young son kicks the ball at Highbury in the 1930s. To the right is George Swindin, goalkeeper (1936-54) and Alex James, centre-forward (1929-37).

On 24 September 2003 Michael Hapgood, Eddie's youngest son, and his sister Lynn unveiled this plaque to Eddie Hapgood on the front of the Community at Heart building. Local artist Mike Baker crafted the plaque which was produced by the Barton Hill History Group in collaboration with Community at Heart, plus other partners.

Above: Family members, friends, local residents and members of the Barton Hill History Group packed Salisbury Street to pay tribute to Eddie just yards from his former home in Ranelagh Street. The unveiling also gained considerable media interest, including pieces on HTV West and BBC Points West. A short speech was given by Barton Hill History Group Committee member Garry Atterton (centre).

Right: Barton Hill History Group members, from left to right: Jim Morris, Jean Brake and Dave Stephenson, beneath the plaque shortly after the unveiling.

Eagle Coaches, Goulter Street. David Cheesley recalls: 'in the early 1970s I made regular visits to Eagle Coaches garage at Goulter Street. The cramped yard housed most of the fleet. Maintenance was carried out in the former stables which had been rebuilt in the 1960s with concrete blocks. At a push two coaches could be squeezed into the building. Mrs Ball, the owner of Eagle Coaches, lived at No. 15 Goulter Street. An advert for Eagle Coaches hung her window. LTE 265C was a 1965 Plaxton bodied Leyland Leopard.

Barton Hill History Group secretary David Cheesley with the late John Ball, the owner of Eagle Coaches, at the Bristol Festival of Transport in 1990. Eagle Coaches was founded by John's mother and father in 1926. John joined the company in 1952 when there were just five coaches and a handful of staff. By 1990 he had thirty coaches and forty staff. He retired in 1993 and died on 31 December 2000. Coach XUF 141 was a 1959 Leyland Tiger Cub restored by John.

three

Around
Maze Street

In the history of Barton Hill, the Maze Street baths, better known as Barton Hill swimming baths, hold a special and unique place. The baths were an important focal point in the life of the community, a key part of the social history of the area. From its early existence, when the washing facilities were seen as just as important as the recreational side, to the days when it was the venue of some of the best swimming clubs in the South West, the Baths were a Barton Hill institution. For generations of East Bristol school kids it was where you went 'for swimming'.

In Victorian days the site of the baths in Maze Street was a saw mill. Maps from the 1880s show a timber yard dominated by a distinctive T-shaped building and numerous sheds. It was this site, to the south of St Luke's vicarage, which was secured by the Bristol Baths and Washhouses Committee for the building of a new set of baths. The planning and construction was a protracted affair but the baths were finally opened (if not completed!) in July 1903.

The heart of the baths was the actual pool (75ft by 30ft).This was surrounded and linked to a rather hotch-potch collection of related buildings. These accommodated the public washhouses and laundry facilities. With its plain, red-brick exterior and tall industrial-style chimney it resembled, from a distance, a small factory. For ninety-four years this venue would be home for ace swimmers and novices plus a meeting place for young and old alike.

Doreen Parsons recalls:
I first went to Barton Hill baths in 1944, when I was ten years old. This was with Avonvale school. I was afraid initially but came to love going and I eventually joined the swimming club. In later years I joined the over-fifties' club and had a happy time going each week. It was a great shame when the council decided to close the baths.

Barton Hill baths were also used by people wanting a hot bath. People could hire a towel and buy soap. There was a strict time limit in the washhouse and attendants would shout at you if you went over time. Additionally, there were also laundry facilities. These services were provided in the days before people had bathrooms and washing machines. On Saturday nights the pool was covered over and people would dance the Light Fantastic. Boxing was also seen there.

The baths were extensively modernised in the late 1960s and in May 1970 they were formally re-opened. However, by the mid-1980s the council began to question the viability of the baths. A reprieve and a new image (Barton Hill Pool) was unfortunately only short-lived. In 1997 it was demolished. By this time a large part of Maze Street had been renamed, becoming part of Queen Anne Road.

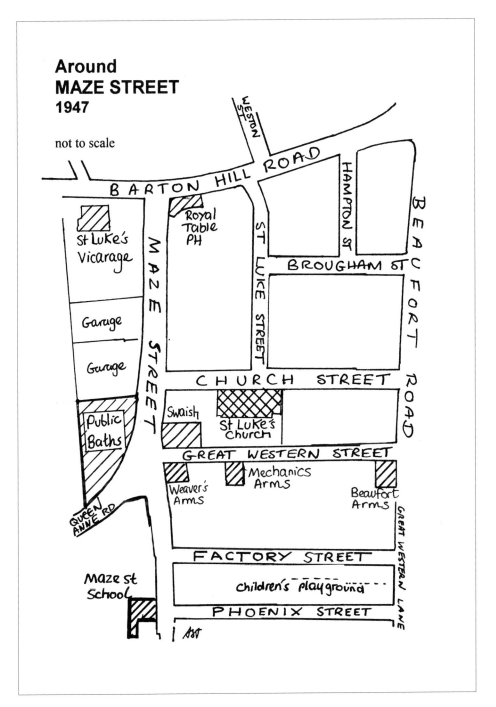

Around MAZE STREET 1947

not to scale

WESTON ST

BARTON HILL ROAD

HAMPTON ST

BEAUFORT ROAD

St Luke's Vicarage

Royal Table PH

ST LUKE'S STREET

BROUGHAM ST

Garage

Garage

MAZE STREET

CHURCH STREET

Public Baths

Swaish

St Luke's Church

GREAT WESTERN STREET

Weaver's Arms

Mechanics Arms

Beaufort Arms

QUEEN ANNE RD

GREAT WESTERN LANE

FACTORY STREET

Maze St School

children's playground

PHOENIX STREET

A map of the area around Maze Street, 1947.

Above: The Lord Mayor in the Memorial Garden, which was created by local people and opened in May 1998. Within its bounds were buried many hundreds of men, women and children who were workers at the cotton factory and members of the Barton Hill community 1846-66. On the right is the First World War Memorial to Barton Hill old boys.

Left: Barton Hill History Group members Garry Atterton (left) and Jack Fryer (right) on Remembrance Sunday, 2003. There are 108 old boys' names on the plaque which was originally at Jarvis Street school. Brought back to Barton Hill by Wally Ball and Johnnie Saysall it was erected at the Settlement before being moved to the Memorial Garden in 2001.

Interior of St Luke's church in the 1920s. The church was built in 1842 with monies for its construction coming from the Church Commissioners, the Great Western Cotton Co., Charles Pinney and Peter Aiken. The land was given by James Duffett of the Barton Hill pottery.

St Luke's vicarage looking from the gardens. This image captures the flavour of what Barton Hill was like 200 years ago – a number of isolated, impressive country houses set in extensive grounds.

Noel Bevan in the grounds of the vicarage. The buildings in the background are in Maze Street, along from the Royal Table. The structure on the left and the late Victorian double-bay terraced houses were demolished to create space around Harwood House tower block.

Jean and Dorothy Wilson outside No. 2 Church Street, Barton Hill, 1950. In the background is Russett's garage and an unidentified lorry.

The tank, minus the water! This is how the interior of the baths looked in its last days. The baths were modernised in the late 1980s and the old balconies and changing rooms were removed.

Interior of the baths, probably taken in the 1920s. Note the galleries which were accessed by an iron spiral staircase which can just be seen at the far end (right). In 1969 a major facelift added a suspended ceiling and orange and blue cubicle curtains! Reports from 1970 noted that modernisation lifted 'the dour, Edwardian look of the baths'.

The baths from Maze Street, 1990s. The jumble of structures attached to the actual pool, as well as the prominent chimney, are clearly distinguished in this photo.

Demolition is under way, November 1997. Note the base of the chimney and that the main pool section still remains intact. Eight years later the site has still not be built on.

Maze Street, 1962. The baths are on the left. In the background is Barton Hill Road. A Ford Popular moves along the 'new Maze Street'.

Mr Harris and swimming team, *c.* 1930.

St Luke's Infants' Day school, Maze Street. A well-proportioned, red-brick structure noted for its large circular end windows. It was opened in 1878 and built on the site of a market garden adjacent to the cotton factory. Miss Collins was the headmistress in the 1930s. After 1945 it was mainly used by St Luke's Sunday school classes.

The year started with very heavy snow; it is 10.15 a.m. on 11 January 1982. Maze Street school is just one week away from demolition. Architecturally, it was quite unlike Barton Hill's other schools. Finally abandoned in the 1960s, it remained rather impressive even in its derelict state.

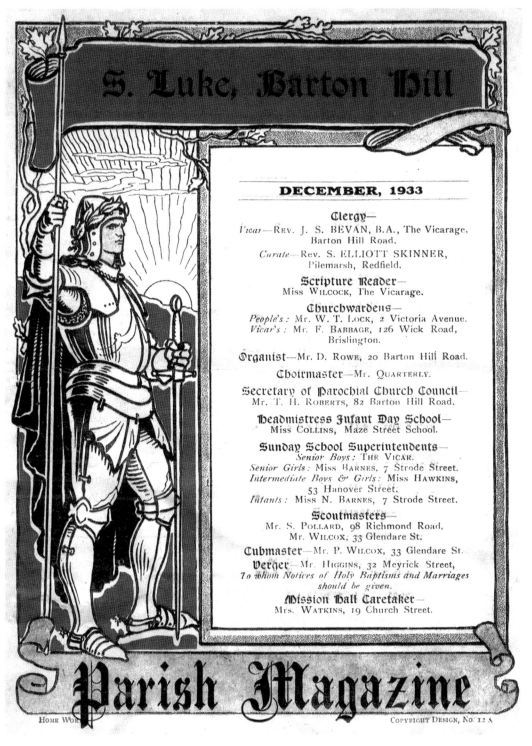

S. Luke, Barton Hill

DECEMBER, 1933

Clergy—
Vicar—Rev. J. S. BEVAN, B.A., The Vicarage, Barton Hill Road.
Curate—Rev. S. ELLIOTT SKINNER, Pilemarsh, Redfield.

Scripture Reader—
Miss WILCOCK, The Vicarage.

Churchwardens—
People's : Mr. W. T. LOCK, 2 Victoria Avenue.
Vicar's : Mr. F. BABBAGE, 126 Wick Road, Brislington.

Organist—Mr. D. ROWE, 20 Barton Hill Road.

Choirmaster—Mr. QUARTERLY.

Secretary of Parochial Church Council—
Mr. T. H. ROBERTS, 82 Barton Hill Road.

Headmistress Infant Day School—
Miss COLLINS, Maze Street School.

Sunday School Superintendents—
Senior Boys : THE VICAR.
Senior Girls : Miss BARNES, 7 Strode Street.
Intermediate Boys & Girls : Miss HAWKINS, 53 Hanover Street.
Infants : Miss N. BARNES, 7 Strode Street.

Scoutmasters—
Mr. S. POLLARD, 98 Richmond Road.
Mr. WILCOX, 33 Glendare St.

Cubmaster—Mr. P. WILCOX, 33 Glendare St.

Verger—Mr. HIGGINS, 32 Meyrick Street,
To whom Notices of Holy Baptisms and Marriages should be given.

Mission Hall Caretaker—
Mrs. WATKINS, 19 Church Street.

HOME WOR...   COPYRIGHT DESIGN, No. 12 S.

Parish Magazine

St Luke's parish magazine, 1933.

Whether by luck or judgement the Royal Table Hotel survived the 'ball and chain', when its neighbouring properties were pulled down. On the exterior Maze Street wall, a small tablet declares that the Royal Table was home to the Barton Hill Swimming Club.

A Ford Anglia travels along Barton Hill Road, 1965. St Luke's vicarage is on the right with the Royal Table straight ahead. The houses on the left, whose back windows overlooked the railway cutting, were pulled down and replaced by a strip of grass.

The old and new Barton Hill, 1965. Powell's chemist with the new landscape beyond. The rear of a Vauxhall Victor can be seen parked in St Luke's Street. Opposite was the shop of Treharne Jones, while Pound's sweet shop was a few doors along towards the Royal Table.

Powell's chemists shop on the corner of Barton Hill Road and St Luke's Street, 1965. Formerly this was Keat's, also a chemist. As can be seen, this was a traditional, small chemist crammed with bottles, pills and all types of remedies.

Left: The University Settlement's George Willis Hall, annexe and floodlit play area, seen here adjacent to a group of properties in Barton Hill Road, which were soon to be demolished, autumn 1965. Across the railway cutting in the background can be seen what remained of Lincoln and Richmond Streets.

Below: A 1965 view from Barton House, with Phoenix House tower block dominating the skyline. Virtually all that can be seen to the left of the tower block would vanish over the following seventeen years. The large building on the left with the apex roof is Maze Street school. Behind that is the roof of Jarvis Street school. The scale of the giant 1894 Folly Lane gas holder can clearly be gauged in this image.

four

Around
Ducie Road

The Settlement has long been associated with Ducie Road. For nearly a century a variety of Settlement buildings have come and gone at the top of the road. However, the Settlement was not about the buildings, but about the people who shaped the place. One such person was the University Settlement's first warden, the amazing Hilda Cashmore.

Hilda Cashmore was born in 1876 at Norton Malreward Court, about six miles from Bristol. In August 1944 her sister Adeline wrote: 'It may have been when we were seven or eight that we heard the story of the children in the cotton mills of Manchester. She seemed to have then onwards a strange sense of responsibility, somehow to make good the miseries and confinement of city life'. Hilda was educated at the ladies' college in Cheltenham and then at Somerville College, Oxford University. She then took an active part in the Chesterfield Settlement before being invited by Miss Marion Pease, the head of a college affiliated to the University of Bristol, to become a history lecturer. It was in those early years that her interest in the Settlement movement, and the ideal of education, started. With colleagues and other bodies such as the Workers' Educational Association, and representatives from trade unions and the Co-operative Society, they began to explore the possibility of a University Settlement in Bristol. The location of Barton Hill was designated a working-class area, but not a slum, although slums were nearby.

In October 1911 the Settlement came into being with Hilda as the very first warden. At first the main business was making friends with neighbours of all ages and showing the community that the Settlement could be a positive force for all the people. The cornerstone would be education and the drive to improve the living and social conditions of the inhabitants.

From the start there was an emphasis on child welfare with a mothers' school and coaching for boys and girls. Kids around Barton Hill soon heard about a big dolls' house, rocking horses, paint boxes, plasticine and books. Hilda loved the children of Barton Hill. One of her friends, Gladys Page Wood, wrote that her compassion for the suffering never wavered. Another friend, Margaret Bonfield, wrote that Hilda had a great gift for friendship which she scattered without stint among the just and unjust.

In 1912 there was a strike at the Great Western Cotton factory. With no wages poverty was strife. Hilda helped the workers and the company in trying to find a resolution. The factory was struggling to make a profit and they brought on wage reduction and cut hours. The factory continued to struggle on for another ten years keeping poverty alive in Barton hill.

Hilda not only worked with the people of Barton Hill, but she was also responsible for the direct relief work of Belgium refugees during the First World War. After working for almost five years, without a break, at the Settlement she was allowed some rest. Instead of taking the rest she needed, she went to Poland to help the peasants affected by war. Hilda also spent four years in India from 1934-38.

It was under Hilda's leadership that the Settlement took on pioneering work. She was courageous, generous, hardworking, shrewd and witty and totally committed to the cause of improving the quality of so many people less well off than herself.

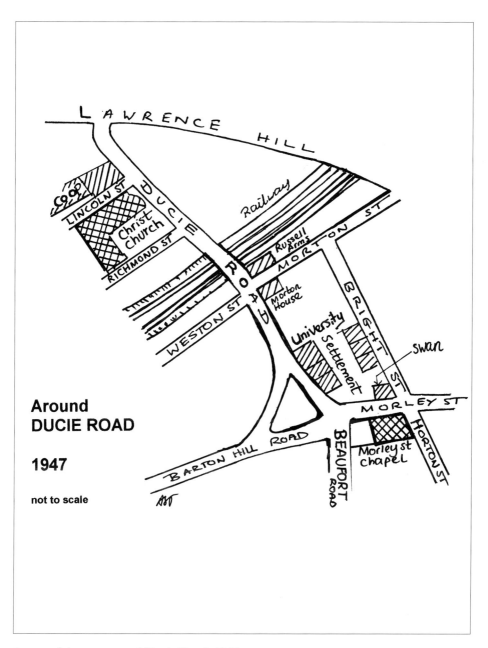

A map of the area around Ducie Road, 1947.

Ducie Road looking towards the junction with Lawrence Hill, 1964. The Co-op on the corner of Lincoln Street dominates the view. This was not a shop but a grocery and dairy warehouse plus a packing and sundries department. The large houses on the right were later sacrificed for a car park.

By 1973 the Co-op buildings fronting Lincoln Street had been demolished but these buildings remained. A camping store used part of the building. Directly opposite a new United Church was opened in 1968.

The Russell Arms on the corner of Ducie Road and Morton Street – a Victorian survivor. The car is, of course, the famous Morris Minor produced from 1948-71. In the late 1970s punk discos were regularly held in the Russell Arms. Barton Hill was the home of punk in Bristol – Barton Hill Rules, OK!

Beaufort House from Ducie Road, 1965. Opened in December 1963 and described at the time as 'sky flats', these were built by John Laing Construction. The neighbouring block, Harwood House, had been opened two months earlier. Reports at the time highlighted the fact that the flats were centrally heated and had radio plus Rediffusion TV. Telephones were not, however, installed!

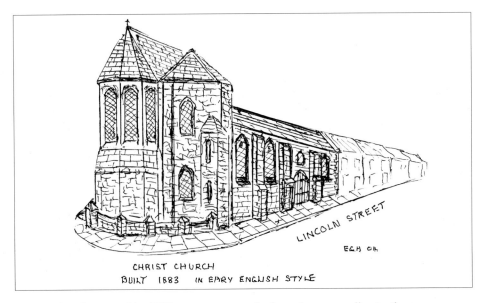

CHRIST CHURCH
BUILT 1883   IN EARY ENGLISH STYLE

Christ Church, opened in 1885, was constructed of rough stone walls, similar to
St Luke's. The main entrance was in Lincoln Street, with an arched double door which
led into the main body of the church. Compared to nearby places of worship, Christ
Church was distinctly 'low profile' in the 1930s. Reverend Bevan of St Luke's took over
the neglected church after 1945, but the church authorities soon made it clear it had no
long-term future. Despite local protests, it finally closed in 1957, being demolished shortly
afterwards.

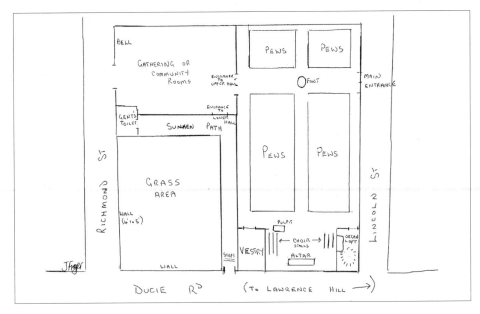

A plan of the layout of Christ Church as drawn by Barton Hill History Group member
Jack Fryer, who, in the late 1930s, lived in Ducie Road. Jack recalls that: 'the exterior was
unremarkable but the interior was quite impressive'.

The wedding of Grace Bevan and John Ancram, mid-1950s. This is outside the main door of Christ Church in Lincoln Street. In the background are the Co-op buildings.

Reverend Bevan is on the right, outside Christ Church. John Bevan was a well-known character in Barton Hill. His period at St Luke's/Christ Church covered the 1930s depression, the Second World War and the start of redevelopment. He was often seen riding around the parish on his bike.

A rare image of the corner of Ducie Road and Morley Street in 1963 before the day centre was built in 1965. In the 1950s a small garden was created replacing the old Victorian buildings on the corner of Morley Street. Note the ornate gateway and low walls.

The top of Ducie Road (the Triangle), late summer 1965. Is the Bartonian on the bench admiring the brand new Settlement day centre or the car, Rootes Group's novel, but ultimately unsuccessful, Hillman Imp?

The old properties in Bright Street, taken from the defunct carriageway of Thomas Street, which was replaced in 1968 by Rowan Court, March 1965. These buildings were part of the University Settlement and the style of architecture is rather unusual for Barton Hill.

Morley Street Methodist Chapel was opened in 1869 and was set well back from Beaufort Road. From 1912 the chapel was home to the 18th Company Boys' Brigade. As the redevelopment gathered pace, boys would go to the Captain, Mr Endicott, saying 'Sorry Sir, we shan't be coming anymore, we are moving away'. In 1959 the BB at Morley Street was disbanded.

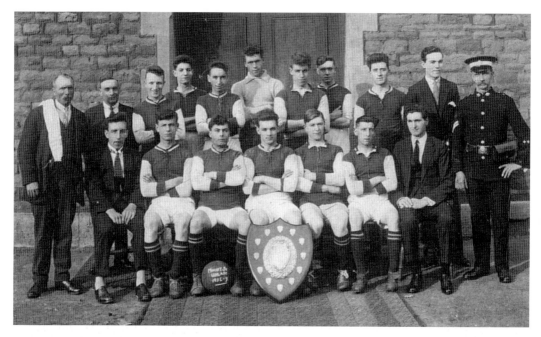

The Morley Street Chapel football team with the shield they won after winning Division 2 of the Bristol Wesleyan and Free Church League. They were Division 1 runners-up in 1930/31. Reg Allen is the player with the shield.

Outside Morley Street Chapel – a group photo from 1940. Among those there are the Portmans (Albert, Joe, Alf and John), Mabel Taylor, Lily Thomas, Olive Powell, Lilly Allen, the Pruetts, Len Bushel, and the Marlins.

Above: The back of the derelict Morley Street Chapel from Horton Street, *c.* 1960. Bright Street is in the distance while behind the camera was Tichborne Street. The lads on their bikes discuss their next move!

Right: Firefighting – the view from the Swan. An unusual image, looking from Bright Street to the roof of the former Morley Street Chapel. The chapel closed in April 1960 and some time afterwards a large fire occurred there. It left the building in a terrible state and eventually it was demolished.

The Triangle and the houses which curved into Ducie Road from Barton Hill Road, 1965. Typical of the late 1860s-70s houses built in the area, they were pulled down between 1966 and 1970 and replaced by the distinctive Barton Green development.

An aerial view of the houses seen in the previous image, with the dwellings of Weston Street behind, 1965. Were these houses really too old and unfit for people to live in?

Richmond Street, 1965 shows that some houses linger on but the tower flats in the background signal the new 1960s landscape. The picture is taken from the wasteland which had, up to a few months before, been people's homes – Richmond Street had once comprised 135 houses. The Bell Inn, a beer retailer, was at No. 25 on the corner with Charlton Street. At Nos 78-80 was another off-licence called the Richmond, not to be confused with the Richmond Hotel.

'All together now'. The compère and the ladies at a Christmas event at the Settlement, 1964.

Mothers and babsters at the Settlement in the 1940s.

It's sandpit time at the University Settlement, *c*. 1950.

Every boy wanted the toy locomotive – it's playtime at the Settlement, *c.* 1950.

The University Settlement children's garden, *c.* 1960.

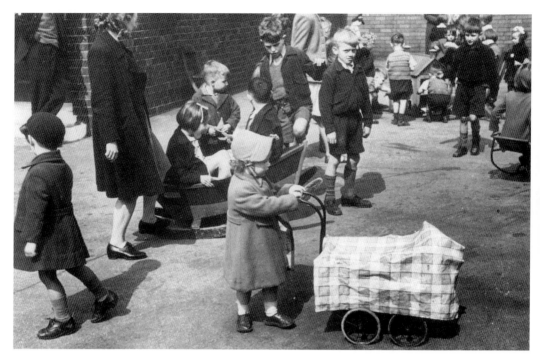

'My go for the pram' – always very popular with the girls, *c.* 1937.

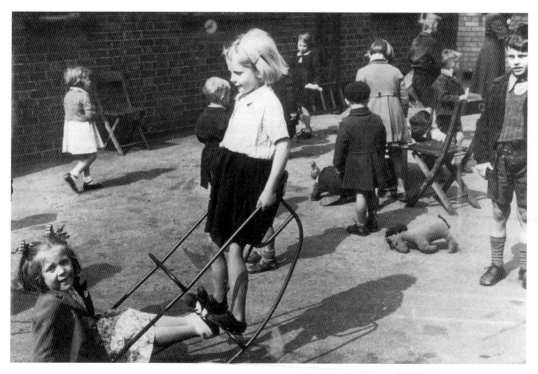

The University Settlement play group area. Note the discarded 'soft horse', *c.* 1937.

'Now girls...' The mothercraft class at the Settlement, 1950s.

We are not sure what is happening here, but apparently it was at the Settlement and worthy enough for a photograph to be taken, 1950s.

Committee meeting of University Settlement workers, *c.* 1930.

A formal team shot. Precise details are unknown although Councillor Cunningham is thought to be present.

The knitting club at the Settlement, 1950s.

Crowning of the May Queen in the 1950s.

The University Settlement football team, note the extra large caps, early 1920s.

The University Settlement team, 1925.

The Whitsuntide festival was an important date in the calendar, 1930s.

The Settlement was host to many events over the years. Do you know who the twins are in this 1950s photo?

Walking to camp at Cleeve, Somerset, 1930s. The camp was established to provide holidays in the countryside for children who had little opportunity to leave their terraced streets.

The University Settlement camp at Cleeve, 1940s. For the leaders of the University Settlement, improving health and fitness were important factors in addressing wider social problems.

five

Around
Marsh Lane

The Great Western Cotton factory dominated the skyline, the economy and the way of life of the people around Marsh Lane for over 100 years. Built in April 1837, the cotton works was the single most important factory in the area. Quite simply, there would have been no Barton Hill without the Great Western Cotton factory. What is amazing is that when the factory closed as a cotton producer in 1924 and a silk producer in 1930 it seemed that it was the end of the story. However, recent research has found that from the end of the silk works until 1968, there was a final chapter that is worth telling of the 'missing years'. This was when the dying giant was still a major force in Barton Hill. The building was not only essential as a shadow factory during the Second World War but also in its final demise it created discussion in the Houses of Parliament!

During July 2004 a letter to the *Evening Post* entitled 'Sad decline of the cotton factory' started with a few quotes from a couple of imaginary friends who remembered the last years of the works in the mid-1960s: 'I am not kidding. It was a dull, depressing-looking building. It was like a prison. It was the Colditz of Bristol.' The response from the letter was excellent and it now provides the information for the basis of this chapter.

In February 1933 the Western Viscose Artificial Silk mills and cotton properties were put up for auction. A copy of the auction describes in great detail the site. It states that the site had extensive and valuable canal footage, frontage to the Great Western Railway and occupied a total of ten-and-a-quarter acres with floor space of 270,000 square feet, with ample water supply and excellent facilities for disposing of trade effluent. The main building was five storeys high, 330ft long and 63ft wide. However, it wasn't sold until October 1936 when the Parker family bought the site. Prior to the Second World War the various mill buildings were re-let.

During the Second World War Beasley, French and Co. of Winterstoke Road, Ashton Gate were detailed to make parts for gun turrets for Parnell Aircraft at Yate. As their site was too small they moved to the cotton works to make perspex cupolas for the gun turrets of Wellington, Lancaster and Halifax bombers, and Sunderland flying boats. The works were known as Bristol Precision. Apparently many of the tradesmen came down from the Midlands, Lancashire and Yorkshire. Some of the women workers came from Devizes, some were servicemen's wives and others were country girls. Jim Sheppard remembers making the tail units and bodies of Spitfires. The Perspex cockpit covers measured about 6ft by 3½ft. Everything came and went in anonymous-looking transport. Jim remembers the work being boring, but the workers were happy as they could chat to each other. It was a long day from 7.00 a.m. to 5.50 p.m. Monday to Friday and alternative weekends 7.00 a.m. to 1.00 p.m. on Saturday and Sunday. There were 45 minutes' unpaid lunch and all this work for just 15s a week!

In the immediate post-war period Coordinated Warehouse and Traffic Services used the site to store drums of Cow and Gate milk powder, animal feed, sacks of sugar and groceries for distribution to stores in the area. Conditions of work were difficult as lorries were constantly unloaded of their heavy goods. There was a product called carbon black (a product of burnt oil) from Albright and Wilson which the warehousemen were paid an extra 1d an hour to unload as the dust seeped through the bags and made them filthy. With so much food around, the rats had a field day!

During the 1950s the comprehensive redevelopment of Barton Hill took place. This involved the clearance of much of the Victorian terraced housing. The owners of the mill wanted the factory to stay and be incorporated into the redevelopment plans. In January 1959 the *Western Daily Press* reported that the 'corporation may buy old mill'. The owners of the old works had offered to sell the building and adjoining land, providing that three industrial concerns were allowed to stay on the site. In 1959 the mill was used, as mentioned previously, as a warehouse by Coordinated Traffic Services. Up to 700 were also employed by Seimen Edison Swan Ltd. Apparently Siemens considered moving from Barton Hill altogether if the factory closed. It seems that the council were torn between shutting down the works and creating large-scale unemployment and purchasing the site for new housing.

In April 1967 the front page of the *Evening Post* led with a story about Association Electrical Industries closing their business. By then 825 people were working there. This proposal caused such a stir that Frank Cousins, the General Secretary of the Transport and General workers' union, came to Barton Hill. Twenty Labour MPs, including the local MP Anthony Wedgwood Benn, met the Minister of Labour Ray Gunter to discuss the issue. However within couple of months the factory was closed. By May 1968 the owners were quoted in the *Evening Post*: 'We are pulling the old building down to clear about four or five acres for the development of a modern factory-distributive estates which will run down to the banks of the feeder canal.' By the end of May 1968 the old mill-on-the-hill was gone forever. Today, a few of the spinning sheds still stand and a spruced-up warehouse. One can only imagine if somebody at the council had the strength of conviction and foresight to have kept the mill. Maybe today we might have had a fantastic working museum reflecting the industrial history of Barton Hill.

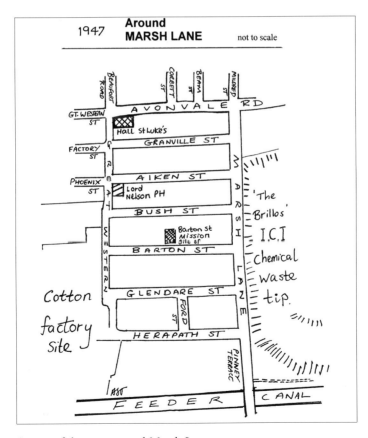

A map of the area around Marsh Lane.

Left: The castellated piers which marked the entrance to the cotton factory, Maze Street, *c.* 1963. From 1838 Barton Hill's new industrial working class would stream though the gates to toil in the giant factory. Two thousand were employed. Soon houses sprung up to satisfy the Victorian convention that workers would live under the shadow of their workplace. Gradually the dwellings would be joined by pubs, corner shops and churches. A new industrial community came into being.

Below: Exterior of the cotton mill. Although over 100 years old at this time, this image gives a fine impression of the power and scale of the works. Nearly everyone in Barton Hill either worked in the cotton factory or knew a relative or neighbour who did. In 1880 concern for the welfare of the cotton workers lead Miss Pease (whose father was one of the owners of the factory) to form a Cotton Girls Club. The cotton girls were described as a 'lively lot'.

The cotton factory's Phoenix Mill from Feeder Road. Small, jumbled workshops, cramped cottages or converted barns were totally inadequate for 1830s cotton machinery and large-scale production methods. Hence buildings such as Phoenix Mill were built by the new breed of Victorian entrepreneurs, to service the increasing demand for cotton textiles.

Marsh Lane Bridge and the factory. The cutting of the feeder canal in the early 1800s changed the character of the district and along its far bank a number of factories were built. The canal was a part of a bold project to improve the Floating Harbour and facilities for the Port of Bristol. In April 1837 the foundation stone was laid for the mighty Great Western Cotton factory.

Barton Street Chapel was built in 1845 in a field next to the cotton factory. In 1877, by then in the middle of Barton Street, it became the Barton Street City Mission.

A rare interior shot of the Mission, 1927. It was severely damaged in the Blitz but sections were repaired. The last services were held in September 1946.

The charabanc outing in the 1920s was the event of the year, whether it was a pub or Sunday school trip. Best clothes were the order of the day and a favoured destination was the Cheddar caves. The charabanc belonged to Charles Russett who operated under the fleet name of Pioneer Transport. Russett's garage was situated in Maze Street next to the baths.

Barton Street City Mission AFC, 1926/27.

Elizabeth Sheeley and Tom Sheeley with friend taken in the backyard of No. 45 Bush Street, 1930s. Bush Street was subject to the 1952 Barton Hill Compulsory Purchase Order and all trace of it was removed.

Glendare Street. This is the 'southern side' of late Victorian houses which survived the redevelopment. The houses on the other side of the road were older, many having long front gardens. These were pulled down under the Barton Hill Compulsory Purchase Order for the building of Glendare House, an eleven-storey block of maisonettes.

A flavour of some of the local businesses in Barton Hill, 1930s.

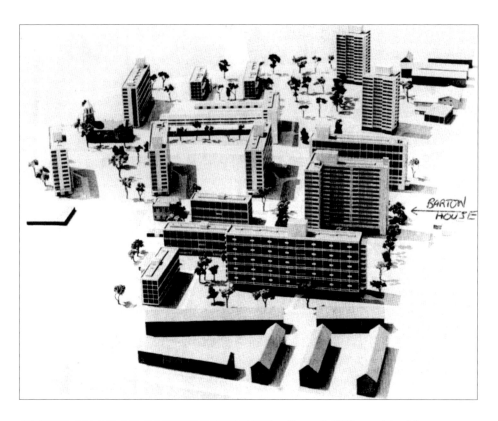

BARTON HOUSE

Above: A 1950s model of the new Barton Hill as envisaged by the Planning Department. In 1951 the University Settlement perceptively noted that: 'pleasant though the general effect was, some of us could not help wondering whether flats would really be liked by the inhabitants and what would happen to the hobbies of people when the little backyards and gardens were done away with'.

Left: An old Bartonian strolls up Great Western Lane, past the Lord Nelson, towards St Luke's, 1965. The new flats dominate the scene but St Luke's survived. So did the Lord Nelson pub on the corner of Aiken Street.

Above: Barton House, fifteen storeys high and, in June 1958, the highest local authority block of flats outside London. It comprised ninety-eight flats, all with central heating. At the time, politicians, architects and planners all agreed that high-rise flats were the answer to poor Victorian housing.

Right: The cover of the programme marking the official opening ceremony of Barton House, Monday 23 June 1958. It marked the completion of the first block of dwellings to be erected by Bristol City Council in the Barton Hill Redevelopment Area.

CITY AND COUNTY OF BRISTOL
HOUSING COMMITTEE

BARTON HILL REDEVELOPMENT AREA
BARTON HOUSE

Official Opening Ceremony

MONDAY, 23ᴿᴰ JUNE, 1958

Above: One of the most evocative images of the district, 1965. Barton House takes centre stage. Off to the left the snooker-table-smooth Netham playing fields (now Netham Park) replaced the 'wild brillos' – this was the unofficial name coined for the chemical tip of the ICI works. In the foreground the Avonvale Road and Granville Street houses stand in the shadow of Bristol's post-war modernism

Left: Looking in the opposite direction towards Corbett and Longlands tower blocks. In the original plans, another two blocks of high-rise flats were scheduled to be built, replacing the houses of Glanville Street seen here. The last of the area's tower blocks, Ashmead House, was occupied in September 1966 and Granville Street survived.

A view from Eccleston House, 1965. The houses in the centre are those of Granville Street. In the foreground are the earlier houses of Manchester Street. These have the old style 'valley gutter' roofs unlike later Granville Street, which was a continuation of the earlier street. Note the Colman's mustard sign and the chimneys of St Anne's Board Mills in the background.

The demolition of Glendare House, 1995. In the mid-1990s Barton Hill's multi-storey blocks were revamped. However, with Glendare, the council stated that because of its original design and layout, refurbishment would have cost twice as much as the other blocks. The block's demolition was helped by a Helen Anglin who assisted smashing a ball and chain through the roof of her former home. Helen said: 'it's exciting, but I am also sad to see the block go because I lived here and everybody was friendly'.

Chetwood and Hartland Houses were two low-rise blocks of flats (five storey) built between Barton House and Great Western Lane. They were demolished in April 2004 in favour of twenty-three new houses and three flats.

Here stand the remains of the Marsh Lane air raid shelters, that provided protection to hundreds of Barton Hill residents during the Bristol Blitz, derelict and forgotten. The tops were removed and the shelter filled in with soil. The shelters ran the full length of Marsh Lane and were built behind the perimeter wall of the ICI waste tip known as 'the brillos'.

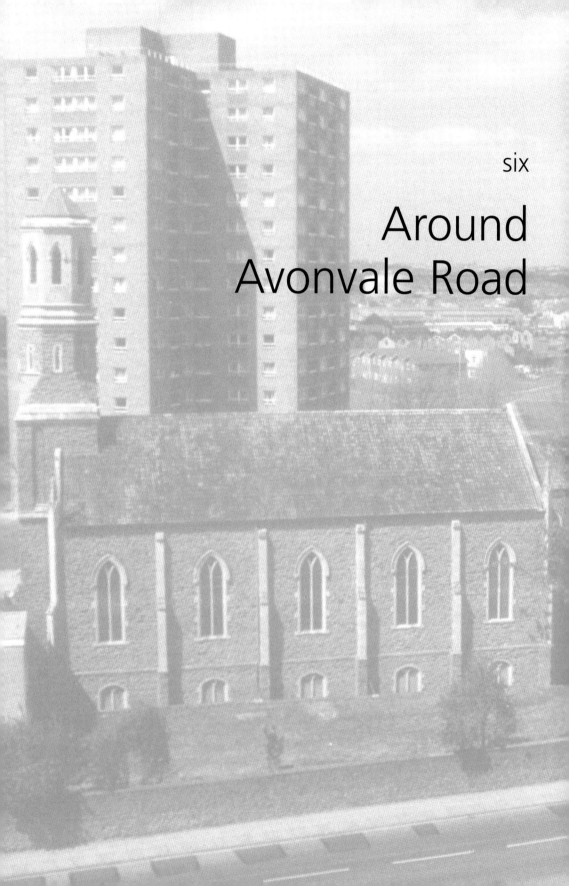

six

Around
Avonvale Road

Avonvale Road links Barton Hill with Church Road and central Redfield. Before the building expansion of the 1890s/1900s what we now call Avonvale Road consisted of two lanes. At the Redfield, Church Road end, was George Lane; sometimes called Sweets Lane. This saw development from the late 1860s when Bethesda church, Orchard Square, Gladstone Street and Clifton Street were built. Past Orchard Square the lane curved sharply into what was known as Pilemarsh Lane. This led to Barton Hill, feeding into Great Western Street. In the 1880s Pilemarsh Lane was still rural in character, bordered by fields, trees and a few large detached houses. In 1884 the St George School Board opened Avonvale school and by the late 1890s, terraces of houses were built along and off of the newly named Avonvale Road. On the 'other side of Avonvale Road, the market gardens stretching down to the Feeder were gradually swallowed by the demands of the huge Netham chemical works. In 1928 Imperial Chemical Industries built a club hall and rooms alongside its works football pitch. This later became home to St Anne's Board Mills Club next to the Netham playing fields.

The Redfield end of Avonvale Road saw demolition in the late 1960s and in 2002 the old Bethesda church of 1868 was pulled down, replaced by flats called St Georges Heights.

In the 1930s a one William Sanigar lived at No. 205 Avonvale Road. Sanigar's importance was that long before history groups and TV history programmes, he produced a number of classic history books on Barton Hill and Redfield and St George.

A result of meticulous research, these well-crafted books are still in the libraries today. His books *Saint George's in the East*, *Houses and People of Old St George* and *Leaves from a Barton Hill Notebook* remain key sources of information for anyone interested in East Bristol's history. Sanigar, an active and strong supporter of the University Settlement, lived to see the start of the Barton Hill redevelopment. He died in 1959.

Andy Jones, current chairman of the Barton Hill History Group:
Sanigar set the standard for writing about local history in East Bristol. His attention to detail, potent imagery and historical skill are of the highest standard. His books, overflowing with description and facts, remain key to understanding the history of our area.

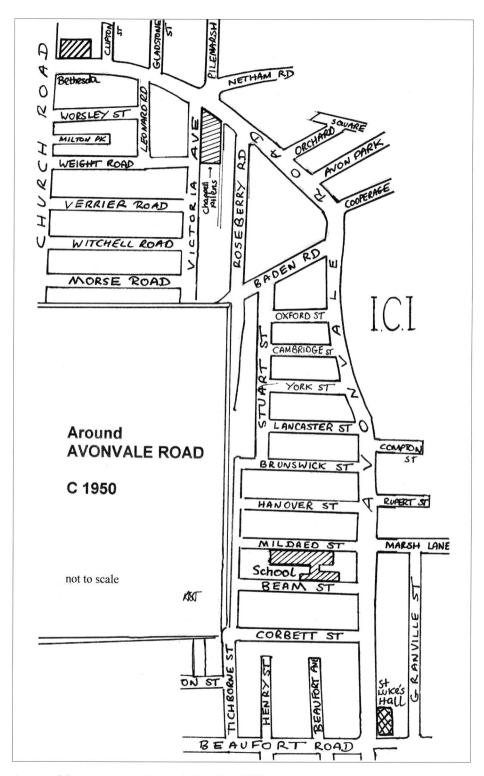

A map of the area around Avonvale Road, *c.* 1950.

The Barton Hill end of Avonvale Road. Before the 1950s this stretch was Great Western Street, complete with houses and three pubs! This view dates from 1983. St Luke's had lost its steeple the year before.

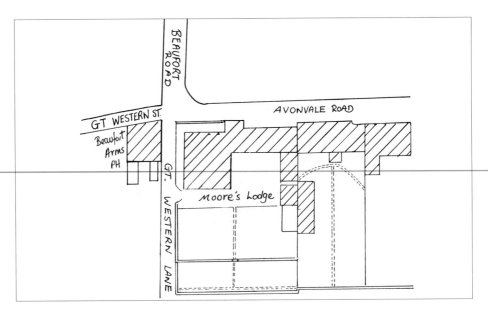

A plan showing Moore's Lodge. William Sanigar states that the Lodge was the early nineteenth-century retreat of a prosperous Bristol merchant called Solomon Moore, whose name is associated with the nearby district of Moorfields. In 1808 this spot was apparently a delightful rural retreat in the parish of St George, a place of fields, narrow lanes and orchards.

St Luke's Mission Hall. This was built on part of the grounds of Moore's Lodge and was opened in 1911. For some years now it has been home of Barton Hill Tenants' Association.

Inside St Luke's Mission Hall. Women of the Bright Hour celebrate Christmas in the late 1940s/early 1950s. In 1965 a new hall for St Luke's was built adjacent to the church but this building managed to survive the ball and chain.

Henry Street was a turning off the busy Beaufort Road. On the corner was the Beaufort
Arms, one of the area's many off-licences. The street party is probably to mark the
Coronation of 1937. Henry Street was part of the Barton Hill which vanished after the
1952 Compulsory Purchase Order.

This is the only picture taken in Tichborne Street that has been found by the BHHG.
The picture is thought to have been taken on VE Day 1945. The street's residents are
assembled outside Scull's newsagents. On the extreme left is Amy Sutton (née Cheesley),
aunty of Dave Cheesley.

Right: George and Rose Charlesworth. George was born on 29 November 1901. He played football for St Philips Marsh adult school and Barton Hill Sports. He signed for Bristol Rovers in 1924 and made twenty-one appearances and scored three goals. He was transferred to Queens Park Rangers in 1926 and made twenty-three appearances and scored three goals. In 1928 he signed for Crystal Palace and made twenty-one appearances and scored eight goals. The Charlesworths owned a fish and chip shop in Beaufort Road.

Below: This evocative image of Corbett Street, 1958, illustrates the changing face of Barton Hill. Note Avonvale school off to the left. What had been a family's front room was transformed into a parking lot; a common feature of the time.

Avonvale school, 1965. In the 1940s this was the entrance to the boys' school. The boys were downstairs, the girls were located on the upper storey. To the left was the boys' playground where underground air-raid shelters were built at the start of the Second World War. The girls and infants used the Mildred Street playground, which also had air-raid shelters.

Mr Parry's class, Avonvale Juniors, 1950s.

Beam Street looking towards Avonvale Road. The houses of Beam Street were demolished from 1956 onwards. The Wellspring Heathly Living Centre was built across the top of Beam Street and was opened in 2004. Note the elaborate brickwork in the arches.

January 1942 and a play is being performed at Avonvale school. From left to right are: Joan Webley, Maureen Clark, Brenda Ward, Doreen Sheeley, Joyce Hallett, June Hayter and Rita Gardiner.

Playtime at Avonvale school in the early 1970s. The Victorian-gothic design of the school contrasts with the tower blocks, which were then barely ten years old.

Lollypop patrol at the top of Beam Street. The school closed, after ninety-one years, in July 1975. The last headmistress was Miss Ena Glide. Rather unusually, the buildings have survived.

The planners saw the land between the tower blocks as 'community areas'. A fascinating snapshot from the late 1960s.

Beam Street looking towards Avonvale Road, August 1965. Corbett Street clinic, on the right, had opened four months earlier. The houses behind the clinic are called Granville Terrace and include the house where the local historian William Sanigar lived.

Ashmead House and Avonvale Road's new parade of shops under construction, 1966. During the rebuilding of Barton Hill, reports from the Settlement stated that public meetings with city councillors and officials were often 'noisy and heated'. Bartonians also did not see eye-to-eye with the authority either about the area of re-building or the proposal to build multi-storey flats. However, by the end of 1966 the redevelopment was virtually complete in the 'central area'.

Avonvale Road looking towards St Luke's (with its steeple intact), Friday 11 July 1980 – in the background is the Folly Lane gas holder which was demolished a year later. Off to the right is Lancaster Street. The cars are a dark coloured Renault 5 and behind a Triumph 2000.

Hadrell's shop was situated on the corner of Avonvale Road and York Street. This shop was taken over by Iris Hadrell in 1974 and she was there for around twenty years. Previously the shop was run by Sam and Doll Jordon. For the Queen's Silver Jubilee celebrations, in 1977, Iris Haddrell and her family organised the street party. The shop closed in the mid-1990s.

Oxford House, No. 112 Avonvale Road. Dating back to the old Pilemarsh Lane days, in 1882 this house was surrounded, not by terraced dwellings, but by fields and trees. Owned by the Brown family in the early twentieth century, it has been used by various clubs since the late 1950s.

The Hop Pole, July 1982. On the left of the pub was a terrace of houses which was pulled down for the 1973 Vetchlea home. On the other corner of Gladstone Street was Capp's, a popular sweet shop. Note the now very rare 1980/81 Ford Escort Mk3.

An architect's drawing of Bethesda Methodist church, which was built on the corner of Avonvale Road and Church Road. It was officially opened on 18 August 1868.

Bethesda church interior; the last service in this building was held in December 1999.

Bethesda Boys' Brigade parade to mark the 50th anniversary of Redfield's 36th company, 1984. At the time Ian Street was Captain of the 36th and Viv Coles and Andy Jones were officers.

The demolition of the 1868 Bethesda church, November 2002. The church relocated across Avonvale Road to its Sunday school building.

St Georges Heights flats were built on the site of the former Bethesda church building in 2003/04. In the 1860s this plot of land was known as Lypiatt's Leaze.

seven

Around
Russell Town

For Barton Hill/Redfield kids growing up in the 1950s, '60s, and '70s, Max Williams' toy shop, near Lawrence Hill railway station, reigned supreme.

Andy Jones recalls:
It was the kind of shop you don't see much today, a small shop crammed floor to ceiling with toys, models, books and accessories. In the days before computer games and electronic wizardry, Max Williams presented a kaleidoscope of the best and latest from Dinky, Corgi, Tri-ang, Hornby and Airfix. With its glass cabinets and olde worlde charm it was a place to browse in a tranquil, unhurried way. If you were lucky enough to have some birthday or Christmas money in the 1960s or '70s there was only one place to head for. It had a unique atmosphere and for me and many others it was simply unrivalled. Going to Max Williams' became a Saturday ritual. Often it was simply to look, but later, as I got older, it was to buy mainly the cheaper Airfix kits – planes, ships or tanks. Max Williams' toy shop was a key part of my 1970s world and even in those days I think we all realised it was a bit special.

Dave Cheesley adds:
It was a shop you could never pass without looking in the windows, to drool over the toys or models you could never afford and the things you might just have enough money for. It was at Max Williams' that I bought my first Dinky and Corgi cars. Later, when I became interested in model railways, I visited the shop at least once a week, buying an item for my layout.

Max and his wife were also busy behind the counter, but never busy enough not to have a chat or give advice. Max was usually beavering away, repairing or testing a loco. Saturday afternoon always saw the shop crammed with people. People came from all over Bristol and further afield because of its large stock and personal service.

It was a great loss when Bristol's best-loved toy and model shop closed forever.

The streets around Max Williams shop were named 'Russell Town' in the mid-nineteenth century. The name was a result of pure Victorian hero worship. The hero in question being the prominent Whig statesman Lord John Russell. He served twice as Prime Minister and by the standards of the day was a reformer in the newly emerging Liberal Party. His role in promoting democracy in the running of British cities caught the imagination of the reformers in mid-nineteenth-century Bristol. The streets of Russell Town – a church, two pubs and school rooms – were East Bristol's tribute to Russell's embrace of parliamentary reform.

In the nineteenth century, politicians were often commemorated by landowners, builders and developers who built the houses. Russell Town could have easily been called 'Gladstone Town' or 'Disraeli Town'!

Streets seen as being in Russell Town included Bright Street and Cobden Street. John Bright was a strong supporter of Russell's position on parliamentary reform, while Richard Cobden worked closely with Bright on political issues. Surprisingly, in the 1920s, the council boosted the fading Russell Town name by renaming Dean Lane in Moorfields. While 'Moorfields Road' was the obvious choice the authorities decided to honour the memory of the former (and to most people rather obscure) Prime Minister. Unassuming Dean Lane became the grandly titled Russell Town Avenue.

Russell Town Avenue was transformed in the 1950s/60s by the demolition of the adjacent houses in Moorfields. However, for many years Russell Town has been dominated by schools – Carlton Park (the original 1900 Moorfields Board school), St George Comprehensive (from 1965) and from 2003, the all new City Academy Bristol.

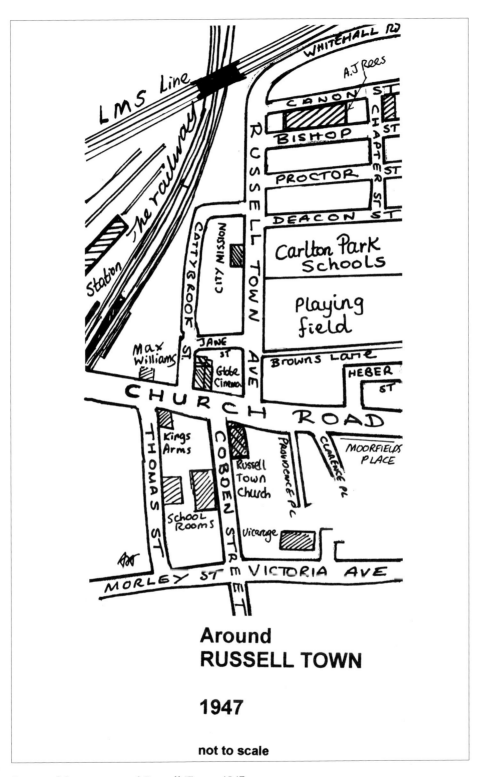

Around
RUSSELL TOWN

1947

not to scale

A map of the area around Russell Town, 1947.

From the top of Cobden Street looking to Avonvale Road, 1961. The high-rise flats, which were to be called Ecceleston and Phoenix, are under construction. Extreme left is St Luke's Mission Hall, while the actual church is on the right.

Russell Town Congregational church is in the process of being pulled down, summer 1976. In November 1966, the *Evening Post* first reported that the church would have to make way for 'tall blocks of flats planned for the area'. The church closed two years later, by which time tower blocks were off the agenda. The structure was used as a store for a while.

Doreen Sheeley and her father Bill on Doreen's wedding day at Russell Town Congregational church in June 1967. In the background, on the corner of Jane Street, is the Globe. This was a famous East Bristol cinema which was closed and demolished a few years before the church.

A rare interior shot of Russell Town Congregational at the wedding of Ron and Doreen Parsons (*née* Sheeley). The building had opened in 1868 and was built of Pennant and Bath stone. It closed after exactly 100 years of worship.

The Thomas Street school buildings, 1963. This small, gothic-style structure was built behind the 1869 Russell Town school which was located in Cobden Street. In the 1950s it was described as Russell Town Handicraft Centre where Mr Moody taught woodwork. Note the impressive height of the masonry arch on the left.

Rawling's furniture shop at No. 12 Church Road still looks like this today. Very much the old-style furniture dealers, it somehow manages to compete with the superstores. Long may it do so.

Until the 1970s Lawrence Hill had a very busy railway goods depot handling coal, cement, bricks and produce for St Anne's Board Mills. In the 1980s it became a storage centre for cars and the home of Arrow Coaches and, later, Ambassador Buses, who eventually went bankrupt. A very derelict Ambassador Leyland National bus is seen here with the old goods shed in the background.

Lawrence Hill station, 1991. A British Rail two-car DMU train arrives with a Severn Beach to Bristol Temple Meads service. In the background is the former goods shed. A cement terminal was established alongside. In November 1997 the shed was pulled down to facilitate the building of a Lidl store which opened two years later.

Max Williams opened a cycle shop at No. 5 Church Road in March 1946. The shop had previously been John Williams & Sons, cycle dealers, but no relation to Max. In 1951 a new shop front was fitted which gave the shop a very modern look for the time. Expansion took place in 1955 with the leasing of No. 7 Church Road (for bikes) followed by the leasing of No. 9 Church Road (for mopeds) in 1957. In 1986 the shops at Nos 5 and 7 were closed and the cycle side of the business moved across the road. Andy Jones was there on the very last day of trading: 'It was 24 July 1993 and I got an Airfix HMS *Devonshire*'.

Max Williams, before the Second World War, was working for Goss's, tailors' merchants in Cumberland Street. He married in the 1930s, Mrs Williams being one of the Witcombe family who owned several shops in town. In 1939, with the outbreak of war, Max became a Petty Officer in the Far Eastern Fleet and was a Sick Berth Attendant on a Dutch hospital ship. He was demobbed at end of 1945 and was then looking around for work to do. As he did not want to go back to the tailoring trade, and his wife had experience in the retail trade, they decided to buy a shop. In March 1946 they bought No. 5 Church Road.

Mr and Mrs Williams ran the toy, model and cycle shop at No. 5 Church Road from 1946-93. The shop was particularly well known in later years for model railway equipment and sold many bits and pieces that could not be purchased anywhere else locally. Mr and Mrs Williams were renowned for their friendliness and knowledge and always gave a first-class service to customers. Mrs Williams died in 1991 and Max died on 29 December 1994.

An advertisement for Max Williams' cycle shop from the 1950s.

Wedding of Mrs and Mrs Williams' son, John Williams, at St Matthews Moorfields church. John worked in the shops at Lawrence Hill and took over the cycle side of the business from his father in 1986 when it moved to No. 18 Church Road. Many customers will remember the late Dave Breddy (with glasses), who regularly served in the toy shop as did John's wife and sister (smaller bridesmaid, to the right).

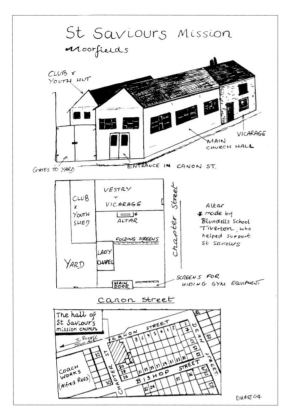

Left: St Saviour's Mission Hall was located in the heart of the Moorfields streets and was originally a mission for St Matthew Moorfields. In 1961 the church sold the building and it became the Venturers Youth Club. Dave Cheesley recalls paying a visit to the youth club with a friend who was a member: 'The only thing I can recall is the table-tennis table and emptiness. Most of the membership had moved away'.

Below: Don't be fooled, this is Russell Town Avenue – the 'St George' refers to St George Comprehensive school. This multi-level building was the successor to the old Venturers Club (see above). In 1980 it was home to the St George school Youth Wing. Andy Jones recalls: 'Wednesday nights – good crowd, good music and after three hours of 'classic table tennis', never had a can of fizzy orange tasted so good!'

An unusual depiction of the Dean Lane City Mission! This building was halfway along Russell Avenue on the left-hand side, approaching from Church Road. A key part of the community of Moorfields, the mission closed when the majority of houses were pulled down in the early 1960s.

In 1914 the University Settlement's Hilda Cashmore moved into a small house in Chapter Street, Moorfields, where on the ground floor a mothers' school was started. The Settlement was concerned by the high rate of infant mortality in Moorfields. In 1945 an Infants' Clinic was opened in Moorfields under Dr Lily Baker. This clinic in Proctor Street served Barton Hill, Redfield and Moorfields and was the first of its kind in Bristol.

Russell Town Avenue, 1962. When the streets in Moorfields were demolished in the mid-1960s only three buildings remained standing. On the 'school side' these were Alfred Rees' coachworks and the Venturers Youth Club. This side-view of the coachworks was exposed after demolition had taken place along Russell Town Avenue. The building on the right was a fish and chip shop on the corner of Bishop Street. The works survived until the early 1970s, the site remaining unused until 1982.

Linda Jones on the playing field, with the Carlton Park school buildings in the background. In the 1920s the University Settlement obtained a grant from the National Playing Field Association and a donation from Settlement benefactor Miss Pease to secure this field, formerly Brown's market gardens. The new playing field was used by the local school, the University Settlement and other local youth groups.

The field was the home ground of the local Boys' Brigade, the mighty 36th Redfield. The lads are in action in this photo from the early 1960s. Heber Street is off right and the field's pavilion can just be seen in the background. This was removed in 1980.

A classic image of Carlton Park school taken from Heber Street. An imposing structure, the school was opened in December 1900 and was then known as Moorfields Board school. By the 1950s it was home to Carlton Park Secondary Modern Boys' school. For the lads of Barton Hill and Redfield, this was their school. In the 1970s a new generation of local lads and girls used this building as part of their school – St George Comprehensive Upper School.

The 1968-75 school blocks of St George School (centre) are sandwiched between the houses of Whitehall Road (top) and the original Moorfields/Carlton Park buildings adjacent to the field. The sports courts, top left, cover the exact site of A.J. Rees' works. St George Comprehensive

School was formed in 1965 and the new blocks were built on the site of Moorfields mass of terraced houses. Ironically the 1960s blocks seen in this picture were demolished before the original Victorian/Edwardian structures.

All: The year 1994 marked the 100th anniversary of St George School, then the oldest state school in Bristol. By this time the whole school was based at Russell Town Avenue. These images capture a memorable day in July 1994 when the school celebrated its 100th birthday. Ten years later the construction of the City Academy transformed the area seen in these photographs.

The old field is being replaced by a state-of-the-art football pitch for the City Academy. This artificial pitch, built to FIFA standards, is made from the latest kind of synthetic grass. A far cry from when rows of potatoes and cabbages were grown on this site!

This building was the former Carlton Park Special school. Built a few years after the main block, to the then latest school design; namely a central hall on a ground-floor level, with numerous classrooms leading off of it on all sides. In later years this was the 'technical block'. A walkway off to the right lead to the Carlton Park exit.

The new sports arena for the City Academy takes shape with the old Carlton Park school building in the background, 2003. The massive arena, which is big enough to hold twelve badminton courts, was officially opened on 25 May 2004 by Sir Trevor Brooking, the former West Ham and England footballer, who scored the winning goal in the 1980 FA Cup Final.

Fifty years ago, the cameraman of this shot would have been stood in Bishop Street surrounded by terraced houses. But this image was captured in the autumn of 2004 with the new blocks for the City Academy taking shape and the houses of Carlton Park in the background. A new era dawns for the area.

Other local titles published by Tempus

Barton Hill

BARTON HILL HISTORY GROUP

Using over 200 photographs selected mainly from the collections of members of the Barton Hill History Group, this pictorial history features fascinating pictures of streets, buildings and factories that no longer exist, well-remembered characters and, importantly, the extensive redevelopment carried out in the 1950s and '60s. This book is sure to prove of great interest to all those with an affinity and love for the old or new Barton Hill.

0 7524 1029 6

St George, Redfield and Whitehall

ANDY JONES, DAVID STEPHENSON, DAVID CHEESLEY AND JILL WILLMOTT

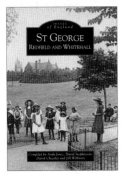

This intriguing selection of over 200 photographs, postcards and engravings illustrates the diverse history of this vibrant area of Bristol. Images of workhouses, municipal buildings and shops are featured and events such as Sunday school parades and Coronation celebrations recalled. *St George, Redfield and Whitehall* draws on the collections of many private individuals to create a valuable pictorial history for all who know these communities.

0 7524 2220 0

Crews Hole, St George and Speedwell

DAVE STEPHENSON, DAVE CHEESLEY, JILL WILLMOTT AND ANDY JONES

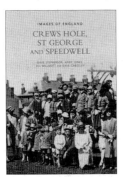

This collection of over 200 archive pictures evocatively captures the histories of Crews Hole, St George and Speedwell in east Bristol. Snapshots of everyday life combine with vistas of the industries upon which these communities relied, particularly the collieries and chemical works whose chimneys towered over this area of the city. This fascinating volume shows the great changes which have taken place in commerce, heavy industry, transport and residential areas.

0 7524 2948 5

Old Inns of Bristol

C.F.W. DENING, WITH A NEW PREFACE BY MAURICE FELLS

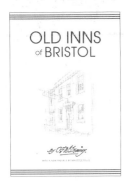

Old Inns of Bristol is a fascinating guide to the historic pubs in the city. First published in 1943, the original book is reproduced here, along with an updated preface by local writer and broadcaster Maurice Fells. This book offers the reader an insight into the life of pubs past and present, from the oddly named Rhubarb Tavern to the dockside pubs with their stories of pirates and smugglers.

0 7524 3475 6

If you are interested in purchasing other books published by Tempus, or in case you have difficulty finding any Tempus books in your local bookshop, you can also place orders directly through our website

www.tempus-publishing.com